THE LIFE OF R.L. HYATT

RONALD HYATT

SOPHOS
BOOKS

The Life of R.L. Hyatt

Published by
Sophos Books
Croydon
www.sophosbooks.com

ISBN 978-1-905669-08-0

Cover design by Tope Enoch
Printed in the United Kingdom

CONTENTS

To Rita, my darling wife.

ACKNOWLEDGEMENTS

I thank my wife, who has loved and cared for me for over sixty-four years. May our love continue to grow stronger as we await the day we enter the kingdom of God to take our eternal rest.

I am deeply thankful to my late parents for all they did for me: To my mother, for caring for me so well and sending me to Sunday school from an early age. It was there I first learnt about our Creator. To my father, for teaching me the importance of kindness. He was a very prayerful man. How I wish I could hear him pray once more! They both raised me to know that there is a living God whom we should love and worship with a pure heart.

I cherish my children, grandchildren, and great-grandchildren: I love you all. Also, my in-laws. You only have one father, but God had one Son, and yet He loved us all and sent Him to die for everyone. He is such a loving God! Put your trust in Him.

My sincere thanks go to everyone who has shown love and kindness over the years, and even now.

I would also like to thank the publisher and all those who helped bring this book to print. May our God bless this company and cause it to prosper and flourish. Many thanks also to Sharon McLean who made the introduction.

Ronald Livingstone Hyatt BA

Chapter 1

INTRODUCTION

It has been my pleasure writing this book, and I must give God thanks for enabling me to do so.

This account was originally compiled as I prepared to mark my 90th birthday. I intended to give it out as gifts to the birthday guests. I had no plans to publish it. However, as the plans for the celebration went on, something happened. I heard a voice say, *"Put your life story in print."*

This book is my response to that instruction. Just as I found great joy in recording these stories, I hope they will be a source of blessing and encouragement to someone navigating this uncertain world.

The world we live in does not offer true happiness. It is filled with troubles, and many are facing difficult times. But I want to encourage you to hold on. There is a living God who watches over us, ready to intervene and deliver. He told Moses, *"I have heard the cry of my people, and I have come down to deliver them."*

He loves us, and He will bless us. One day soon, things will turn around, and your heart will be glad.

Chapter 2

Life After Birth

I was born on Friday, 20th October 1933. According to my mother, who was then a young 21-year-old, she went into labour on Wednesday, 18th October, but did not give birth until Friday, noon on the 20th October 1933.

When I was told of the hard time she had, my response was, 'Maybe I did not want to come into this wicked world!'

As our family history goes, I am of mixed race: part Jewish, part European, and part African.

My mother's father, David Kerr, was a Jewish estate owner in Jamaica during the 17th and 18th centuries. He had three children: two sons and my mum, who was his only daughter. Unfortunately, he died when she was about three years old, so she did not get to know him. Her mother raised her. Out of the two brothers she had, she only met one who was a police officer, stationed in Spanish Town (the former capital of Jamaica). The other brother was a Captain who had his ship and probably travelled a great deal.

Much later, as a young man living in London, I once saw a boat ship with the name 'Kerr' on it. That was my mother's surname, and I could not help but wonder if there was a family connection.

My mother grew into a very attractive and caring young woman. She did not fall pregnant from a casual encounter. She and my father were in a committed relationship and were engaged to be married. As he already owned a house, she moved in with him. Sadly, several events unfolded that led her to move out after I was born.

Though she had little, she did her utmost to ensure we always had a good meal and that I was well looked after. Times were often hard, especially as she raised me on her own, and for many years, my father did not provide child support.

My mother told me how much I loved being in water whenever I was bored and wanted to cause trouble. She would simply get the bath pan with water and put me in, sometimes for hours. That also gave her the chance to get more work done around the house.

My earliest memories go back to when I was three years old. I accompanied family members to visit my mother's youngest sister in the hospital about nine or ten miles away from home. I remember that my father was one of the gravediggers at her funeral.

In Jamaica, when someone dies, we observe a tradition known as 'Nine Nights'. During this period, family, friends, and neighbours gather to celebrate the life of the departed. I recall that during one of these gatherings, when it was teatime, all I wanted was a cup of coffee and a piece of hard bread. I still remember the colours of my pyjamas: red and blue.

I also remember some of the key issues of the day, particularly the public uproar that followed King Edward VIII's decision to marry Wallis Simpson, the American divorcée, in 1936. One of my cousins, a devoted royalist, was furious when she read about it, just like most people at the time.

I also recall my great-grandmother's death in 1938. I even remember one of the songs that was sung at her funeral: *When the roll is called up yonder, I will be there.*

As a child, I used to see ghosts a lot. At the time, we called them 'Duppy'. They were stiff, headless beings that moved around a lot at night.

I began attending Sunday school at the age of three. A young lady about four years older than me would come for me every Sunday morning, and we would walk there together. Those classes left an early impression on me about the existence of a God who created and loved us, although at the time, I barely understood the significance.

As I've mentioned, my mother did not have much, but she was determined that I would not be deprived of the basics, one of which was education. At the time, a local woman ran a preparatory school for children. It cost two old pence per week, eventually increasing to six old pence, which was a lot of money for a single mother. Yet, somehow, she always managed to pay it.

In those days, children would attend the preparatory school until they were old enough to enrol in the elementary school at age seven. In my case, I had two cousins who were teachers at the elementary school, so

I was admitted early, at six and a half years old. Around that time, in 1939, the Second World War broke out. On the day war was declared, the local Methodist church rang its bell loudly to alert the community.

The war affected us in Jamaica, just as it did in England and elsewhere. There were shortages, blackouts, and the skies were often filled with aeroplanes. The Americans, who joined the war later, had an airfield about fourteen miles from our district, in Rio Bueno.

According to my mother, I was quite good-looking even as a young child. My hair was so long that it cascaded down my back. She cried the day my father cut it off. I also seemed to be a favourite with people around. I remember many mothers with daughters loved having me around their homes. It didn't seem unusual then, but looking back now, I'm reminded of a Jamaican saying: *"Put two and three together!"*

My father's side of the family was from Africa. When the Europeans went to Africa and took our fore-parents into slavery, many of those Africans came from royal families. They gave them good jobs, such as head supervisors and other high positions in leadership.

This made me conclude that my grandfather was one of such people, and that was why he was the head sugar tester in the cane factory where he worked. In today's terms, this would be a high position.

The European owner of the factory allowed my father to live with their family, but they did not send him to school. If my father had been able to get a good education, he would have made a very good teacher. He was a just and very wise man. He hated injustice and was very kind to others. This was most probably how he came about the name, 'Hyatt'.

I once researched the name and traced it to an aristocratic family in Hertfordshire, England. They remain closely knit and even have their coat of arms.

Many years later, I was hospitalised as an adult. The man in the bed next to mine was African, and I noticed he bore a striking resemblance to my father, grandfather, and uncle. I discovered he was from Ghana, West Africa, and descended from a royal family. When one of my sons visited me in the hospital, he also noticed the resemblance. We formed a close bond during our stay.

When he was about to be discharged, I had two ripe bananas and I gave him one, telling him that when he met his family, he should tell them he saw one of his family members, who is a Jamaican, who had two ripe bananas and gave him one!

As you may know, there are also hotels all over the world with the name Hyatt. I do not know if I am related to the family that owns them, but it would be very nice, knowing that I may be able to get a five-star room on the cheap! One of my sons went to a hotel in America, and when the staff saw his name, they treated him with unusual deference.

Many of us may never know who we are related to, so let us treat everyone with kindness and respect. There are probably many people in the UK to whom I am related, but whom I may never meet.

As a child, we lived in a district called Duanvale, Trelawny. In the 1930s and 1940s, there was no public transport, so we walked everywhere.

I used to walk to Clarke's Town in Trelawny, Jamaica, which was a five-mile journey from my district, to do some shopping. At the age of ten, I walked ten miles to visit my mother, who was then hospitalised in the Falmouth Hospital. Between the ages of ten and twelve, I carried breadfruit on my head and walked eight miles to sell it at the market in Duncans, Trelawny. I also walked sixteen miles to Rio Bueno Town to visit an aunt.

At some point, my mother moved to live in upper Trelawny, Jamaica, and I had to walk 4 miles to school every day. I had to get out of my bed, go to the spring to fetch water (there were no pipes provided locally) before I could go to school.

My grand-uncle in my district owned a vehicle and had a PPV licence to transport passengers to Falmouth, Montego Bay, or Kingston — but he only made these trips on certain days.

While living in Upper Trelawny, I enjoyed swimming with other neighbourhood children, despite not being a strong swimmer. I still do not know what got into me, but one day, I decided to go on my own. I went into the river and found myself at the deep end. I went down once, and then a second time. It had to be God who saved me from drowning and helped me get out of that water that day!

In 1936, we heard that my father was getting married to another woman. The wedding was held on a Sunday, and although I wanted to attend, my mother refused to let me go. The next day, I visited my father, who gave me a slice of wedding cake to take home. When I gave it to my mother, she angrily threw it away. As I mentioned before, she was of Jewish descent and not one to be trifled with.

Little did I know that I would soon have to live with my dad and his wife - an experience that turned out to be traumatic for me.

My father was not giving my mum child maintenance, so she decided to take him to court. He was ordered to pay a weekly amount as child support. Still, he failed to keep up with the court order. My mother then came up with a plan: she would go to work while I went to live with him and his wife. I was about six at the time.

My life took a sharp downward turn. His wife treated me poorly. I later discovered it was because my father had told her he should have married my mother instead. Her treatment left such a mark on me that, even as a child, I resolved that any woman who bore me a child would be the one I married.

My mother was working as a housekeeper elsewhere, but when she heard what was happening, she returned home and took me back.

When my father still refused to give her any support to enable her to give me a decent quality of life, she took him back to court again. She later told me how the judge told him off and he cried like a baby. He begged her not to take him back to any court, and that he would do his best to support us.

Despite all that was happening, I loved my father. I could have turned against him, but I would not do such a thing. We are told in the Bible to honour our mother and our father that our days may be long upon the land.

I did very well in school and had a natural aptitude for learning. I was the type of student teachers could count on to get my sums right. I also excelled in writing and was considered an all-rounder, strong in Mathematics, Geography, Science, and English. There were four of us in the class who consistently delivered the correct answers.

Unfortunately, my educational journey was cut short by the norms and expectations of the time. At 14 and a half, I was summoned to the headmaster's desk and informed that my time at school was up, as I had started at six and a half. I was in Class Five and doing exceptionally well, but I had no choice in the matter. It was a major setback.

At that time, education from the preparatory to the elementary level was private. Children remained in school until about 16. If your parents were well-off and you passed the Sixth-Class exam, you could go on to university or college. But higher education was expensive, and only the wealthy could afford to study in Europe.

My original ambition was to either join the police or the army, or to raise capital and go into business. I wanted to become a millionaire by the time I was thirty-five. Having seen how hard my father laboured in the fields to survive, I knew I didn't want that life for myself.

CHAPTER 3

POST SCHOOL & MEETING CHRIST

After I left school, I was apprenticed to a shoemaker to learn the trade of making and repairing shoes. But I didn't enjoy the work. This might have been worsened by the fact that the owner of the workshop was neither a particularly skilled shoemaker nor did he use machines. Everything was done manually. Later, I was sent to another shoemaker who was more skilled and equipped.

Until then, I was like every other young man in the district. But something happened that changed the entire trajectory of my life.

On the 1st August 1951, the district was having a fairground party. This was a public party where everyone came together to celebrate the freedom of slaves who were brought from Africa to Jamaica to work.

A dance party was planned for that night, and I was there waiting for the night to fall, when I would join everyone else to dance the night away. I was also hoping to find a girlfriend that night.

While I waited, I watched as the crowd and the excitement increased. People kept streaming into the grounds to take part in the dance and all the fun that night. As I looked at the gathering of the people, I found myself thinking, *"If God should come now, we would all go to hell."*

I had no idea where that thought came from, but clearly, God heard me. The desire to take part in the party suddenly left me. Instead, I turned and made my way to the Pentecostal church on our street.

On the way, I ran into my mother, who was a well-known dancer in the area. She asked, "Why are you leaving so early?" and encouraged me to go back to the party. I agreed, mainly because I hoped to get some money from her, but I still intended to go to church that night.

As soon as I could, I slipped away from the party and went to the church. I found a seat at the back, not realising someone had seen me come in. A young lady who used to take me to Sunday School as a child came over and invited me to the altar.

At first, I hesitated. I didn't have a job, and I felt I needed to get some decent clothes before making such a public decision. But the young lady began to pray, and eventually, I went forward. As I knelt, I heard a voice say, *"Seek ye first the kingdom of God and His righteousness, and all these things shall be added unto thee."*

I began to pray. It felt as though the weight of the entire world was on my shoulders. I cried out, *"Oh, Jesus, come into my life! I promise to serve you all of my days. I will never leave you if you guide me to the end."*

After some time, I felt incredibly light. I knew, without a doubt, that something had changed in me. Afterwards, everybody in the district seemed to notice that something had changed and I was a different person. The dear sister who prayed with and for me that night became my mentor. She supported me and encouraged my growth in the faith.

About two weeks after I invited Christ into my heart, I gave my testimony during a service. When the service ended, a young man who had been watching approached me and said, "I give you six weeks and you will leave the church." This happened on the 1st of August 1951. Here I am, nearly 92 years old, and still serving my God! Of course, without His help, I just would not have made it.

Sometime later, I was elected youth leader at the church. One night, we had a visiting minister, and the deacon asked me to lead the service. I did. The preacher was anointed, and a revival broke out! Many people were saved that night.

The church began encouraging me to consider the ministry. I gave it serious thought, but life took a different turn.

A few weeks after my salvation, I had an unforgettable dream. I saw myself in heaven. The beauty of the place was beyond words—unlike anything on earth. The peace, the calm, the rivers... I didn't want to leave. But suddenly, I was back in my bed, and I saw a very stout man walk away from me. He said, *"If you remain faithful, you will spend eternity with Me."*

Earlier in my school days, I never looked for fights, but if anyone started one with me, they were certainly going to get one!

There was a boy in our district—my cousin on my father's side—who, along with his younger brother, was a known bully. One Saturday morning, the two of them picked a fight with me. During the scuffle, I managed to trap the older brother's head between my legs and held him there while using my hands to fend off the younger one.

While this was going on, a crowd gathered to watch the fight. When we were eventually parted, the older brother threatened, *'Wait until next time!'*

'The next time, I will break your neck!' I responded.

Everybody roared with laughter. My mother, who had been in the crowd too and was standing by, said to me, *'I am proud of you'.*

After that day, he never again picked a fight with me. But it was because of him that I eventually decided to leave the district.

Coincidentally, we had become apprentices at the same workshop. One day in April 1956, while we were working, he began insulting me with mean remarks. Right there and then, I decided I no longer wanted to live among such evil-spirited and jealous people. That day, I made up my mind to leave the countryside and move to the capital city, Kingston.

Not long after, I moved to Kingston and found a job in a more modern shoe-making shop, where machines did most of the work. I found it far more interesting than my previous experience, but even this was short-lived.

Soon, the Jamaican government, in partnership with the American government, selected workers to assist with the harvest in the U.S. during the war. In June 1956, I was called to undergo a medical examination. I passed, and I was sent to America to work on the farms.

I saw it as an opportunity to earn money and return to Jamaica to start the business I'd always dreamed of.

Being in America was an eye-opening experience. I was the youngest among over 200 men who boarded the plane. We worked on plantations, harvesting crops. It was here that I faced realities that shaped me and taught me lasting lessons.

Thank God I was a born-again Christian. On the Friday when we received our first pay, some women offering sexual services came into the camp.

Of the 200 men, only four of us did not join the queue for their services – I, another Christian man, and two non-Christians. Watching from my window, I was shocked by the line of men. I was the youngest in the camp.

Later, I was transferred to Florida to help with the orange harvest. This camp housed 80 men and had communal bathrooms. One of the young men had unusually large genitalia, something I'd never seen before. I remember thinking, *"I hope no female relative of mine ever ends up with a man like that."* As far as I knew, only animals had such large body parts.

We shared a bunk bed. He was on the lower deck, while I was on the top deck.

God said he will deliver His own, and I can assure you, He certainly does.

The camp manager was Jamaican, and when he heard I was a Christian, he invited me to share his room. The same week I moved out of the room I shared with the young man, the sex workers started coming in.

One of them was a very young woman whom I heard was a teacher. During one of our trips, I learnt that the man with whom I used to share a room had slept with her. Because of his size, he caused her serious internal damage, and she later died. It broke my heart to hear such a thing.

After a year, I returned to Jamaica. My father wanted me to migrate to England, but I wasn't interested keen on the idea. Two weeks later, however, I changed my mind. When I told my father, he was overjoyed. He went to Kingston and booked a ticket for my brother, Donald, and I to travel to the United Kingdom.

We departed on Monday, 26th August 1957, travelling by sea to Spain, then to France by train. From there, we took a ferry to Southampton, and finally, a train to Victoria Station in London, arriving on 10th September 1957.

Chapter 4

Life in England

As soon as we arrived at the Port in England, the culture shock began. Some of those who travelled with us on that trip returned to Jamaica immediately. At first sight, they did not like the cold, war-torn country and did not think they could cope.

On the first morning after our arrival, I went for a walk around London. It was not a pleasant sight at all. The bomb sites from the war were still visible, and to make matters worse, the people were not particularly friendly. We had been invited to come and help rebuild the United Kingdom, yet we were treated like second-class citizens. Some children would even come to us, curiosity written all over their faces. They expected to find tails behind us because they thought we were monkeys!

I had travelled with my pocket money, and we were advised on the ship that it would be better if we changed our notes into silver coins. So, we changed it all into one and two shillings, which turned out to be quite unnecessary (Jamaica and England were using the same currency at the time).

Upon arriving in London, I went to the post office to change the silver coins into notes, and the postman nearly called the police on me. He could not understand how I had so much money - about eight pounds.

The next challenge we faced was securing employment, and that was no small feat.

We went to the Labour Exchange and were sent to factories where there were reported vacancies. Interestingly, once we arrived, we were told, "No vacancy!"

When we returned to the officers at the Labour Exchange and relayed what we had been told, they were just as surprised as we were. They knew those factories had openings. Of course, the real issue was that they did not want to see any Black faces.

There were some places we just could not go because we were black, and there were others we could. Only a few organisations like the British Rail, Road and Transport and the Post Office were employing Black and Indian workers.

The English people did not want to do what they saw as dirty jobs like sweeping the streets, working in the factories, or even in the hospitals. The Africans and West Indians, on the other hand, were glad for the opportunity to get trained as nurses. Even then, the wage paid to nurses was very poor; they received about £2.00 per month after deductions of living costs. Many of the nurses left and went to work with other companies, such as the Post Office and London Northern Transport.

Finding accommodation was just as difficult. You had to have lived in the Country for 30 years before you could get a Council house to rent in those days. If you saw a sign that read "Room for Rent," it often came with the warning: *No Irish, No Blacks, No Dogs.* Luckily, there were a few people, mostly Africans, who wanted to buy houses and had the means to. The house I ended up living in, for instance, was owned by a Nigerian. Of course, property was cheap at the time. For instance, a large house could cost around £1,000. Not many people were able to buy homes then. Yet, some Africans and West Indians managed to save enough to purchase properties here and there.

When I moved in, I shared a room with another young man named Anthony Maddix. He was also a Jamaican, but had been in England ahead of me. Room-sharing was common at the time because the weekly rent was rather high, so splitting the cost made it more manageable.

The discrimination we experienced was not limited to the workplace, residential apartments, the shops or the streets. Sadly, even the established churches were not happy to see us in their buildings.

I had been christened in the Methodist Church in Jamaica and attended Sunday school there as a child. My father even wanted me to train as a Methodist minister. I was pleased to discover a Methodist church in New Cross, London, and decided to attend a service one Sunday. What I encountered was deeply disheartening. The message was clear: *You are not welcome. Don't come back.*

I never returned to that or any other Methodist church in England after that experience. It was a very sad moment. I firmly believe that all churchgoers should be happy to welcome everyone - black, pink, yellow, white, or brown. We are all God's children.

Working and living in England was far from easy, with low wages and poor working conditions. I once worked on a building site as a labourer, and I was given the chance to do the painting. The foreman saw that my work was so professional that he dismissed the painter and let me continue, but still paid me a labourer's wage.

As a born-again Christian, there were certain places I could not go and pastimes I could not indulge in, unlike many of those around me. I eventually found a born-again Christian church, which I began to attend, though I still wasn't completely happy.

I tried to improve my situation by enrolling in night school, hoping to enter a proper profession. However, I had to give it up. Classes began at 6 pm., and my workplace also closed at 6 pm. Sometimes, I even had to work overtime.

I also enrolled in a driving school. If I had passed and obtained my licence, I would have returned to Jamaica. In those days, one could secure a good job as a professional driver, perhaps even working for a wealthy individual. Sadly, I didn't pass.

"Trust in the Lord and lean not on your own understanding."
Proverbs 3:5

Chapter 5

A Good Wife

My father had about ten children with three different women, but I am the only one alive today. You may recall that I made a pledge as a child: any woman who bore a child for me would have to be my wife. I faced innumerable temptations from women wherever I went, which could have jeopardised that pledge, but God helped me. I will give a full account of that in another chapter.

Around January or February 1960, I began to ask the Lord to bless me with a good Christian wife. I had no one to talk to or share my heart with, and there were places I could not go to socialise. Many people went to pubs and dance halls, but as a believer, those places were not for me. Life became quite lonely. So, I turned to God and prayed, *"Please provide a wife for me..."*

I was 24 years old at the time.

My friend and roommate, Maddix, invited me to a baptismal service at his church, Church of God of Prophecy, a Pentecostal congregation. After the service, we were chatting outside when two young women he knew walked by, shook our hands, and continued on their way.

At this point, my friend turned to me and asked, *"You see that young sister? Do you love her?"*

"Which one?" I asked

"That short one," he said, pointing to one of them. *"She is hard to get, but if you can get her, you will get a good wife!"*

He added, *"If you want to meet her again, I can make the arrangements with her for you. She's very busy in the church."*

I learnt her name was Rita Adassa Morgan. He arranged for us to meet on the first Thursday in May 1960.

I met up with this young lady and walked her home to her father's house. It was the first time I'd stayed out that late since moving to London, but it was well worth it.

On getting back home, my roommate was up waiting to hear the news of my meeting with her. I told him immediately, *"I've met my wife."* I thought she was so cool! What struck me most was that she wasn't interested in worldly goods. In those days, many girls would want to know what you had - money, house, possessions. I knew girls who wouldn't have married me without those things. But she didn't care about any of that. I just knew she was the one.

We continued seeing each other, and I felt increasingly drawn to her, especially because of the way she spoke and how she spoke to me.

After a few weeks, she told me to go and see her father. I asked, *"How come you are telling me to go and see your father when you have not said 'Yes' to me?"*

She insisted, *"Go and see my father."*

So, on the third Sunday in June 1960, I set out for her home. The road that led up to her father's house was quite a long stretch, and as I was walking up that road, I suddenly remembered a dream that I had between January and February 1960.

In the dream, I had gone to ask a man for his daughter's hand in marriage. As I walked up that very road, I realised it was the same one from my dream. A man was working in the garden, just as in the dream, wearing the same clothes. Rita came out wearing the exact same dress I had seen in the vision.

Her father agreed to the marriage, and we set our wedding date for 1st October 1960, just five months later. In my dream, he was a baker. However, it was his wife, Rita's stepmother, who baked a beautiful cake for our wedding.

We came from different churches, but once the news got out, her church family held fasting and prayer meetings for us. They prayed that our coming together would be blessed and successful.

As the wedding day drew near, I knew I needed a place of my own. I didn't want to live in my father-in-law's house. I found a place that promised a room, but just two weeks before the wedding, they said it wasn't ready. I was so worried that I began losing weight. Where would I take my bride?

We got married on 1st October 1960, and it was one of the biggest weddings of the time. We had about two to three hundred guests attend the ceremony. Rita's church was against the use of wedding rings, but we had already bought one and went on to exchange vows with them as symbols of our commitment to each other. Some people from her church boycotted the rest of the ceremony, probably because of this. About half of those who attended the wedding ceremony did not show up at the reception party.

We were able to finance the wedding with our savings. I also had some savings with my father in Jamaica. Rita's stepmother baked the wedding cake, and there were about two to three hundred guests at the reception: people from her church, my church, and friends came from different places.

After we got married, we moved into a basement room. If you visited us, you had to be prepared to sit on the bed. We were there for a few weeks before moving into the room that had earlier been promised to us.

Back then, it was expected that born-again Christians would start a family immediately, but my wife was unable to conceive due to a medical issue. She needed a major operation before she could have children. I had to sign a consent form before they could carry out the operation, but I could not sign it because I was scared she might die.

By the time I got to the hospital, I was told Rita was already in the theatre, and she had signed the form herself.

Thankfully, the operation went well, and she was discharged. Not long afterwards, she became pregnant, and we were blessed with our first child, a baby boy named Horace. We had waited three years.

Now that we had started a family, our accommodation was no longer suitable. I decided we wouldn't have another child until we had our own house.

Not long after we had our first child, however, my wife told me she was pregnant again. I said, *"No way am I gonna allow any more children to come and live in a rented home!"*

With the help of a friend, I was able to buy a house.

We went on to have six children: Horace, Andrea, Karen, Andrew, Coretta and Mark.

Raising six children was by no means a walk in the park, but God was faithful. The devil tried to destroy the family, but those who trust in the Lord will never fall. We relied on God every step of the way, and He always came through.

From the beginning, I wanted to marry a born-again Christian because I wanted us to raise our children the right way. We ensured they started Sunday school from age three, sometimes even younger, so they were raised in church. One of my fondest memories is going to church with them.

Our children were very bright kids in school as well. They always got good reports.

However, the devil has a way of testing people, like he did to Job. He wanted God to let him test Job and see what he would do, but nothing he did to Job could make him curse God. He said, *"Even though he slays me, yet I will trust him."*

It was difficult, because though our children were raised in a Christian home, they encountered a very different world at school—teachers who weren't Christian, children from all kinds of backgrounds. These things can influence young minds.

The first book that I published was "Walking with God in This Troubled World". Today's world is even more troubled. In today's age, it would be very difficult to raise six children as we did then. I'm not sure I would want to have more than one or two children.

Even then, and for various reasons, it was not very easy raising six children. My wife had to stop working to look after them. Back in those days, she could do that. In today's world, it would be tough.

We brought them up in a Christian home and tried to teach them about God's goodness. Though there were many challenges, they are slowly turning to the Lord, one by one, because of the foundation we laid.

Parenting is even more challenging now, with all that is going on in our schools and society. What can we do? We have to walk with God, talk with Him, keep our eyes on Him and never look back.

One of our sons gave us much trouble at school. No matter where we enrolled him, he couldn't settle. Croydon Council couldn't understand why, so they arranged a test. The result? He had one of the highest IQs in the country.

We were told the council allocated £18,000 to send him to a private school, but he would have to decide. He rejected the offer and told us he was not going, and that it would be like sending him to prison.

He told me, *"Dad, I don't have to go to the university to be a millionaire."* And, to God's glory. he has done well for himself.

One of our daughters also gave us many challenges. If not for God's grace, we might have ended up in prison. Today, that same daughter is a head pastor in her local church. As we say in Jamaica, *"What don't die, don't call it Duppy!"*

This is my encouragement to every parent: even if your children give you difficulties, keep trusting God. He will work in His own time. Please, parents, pray for your children. The devil seeks to kill and destroy. Rebuke him! Tell him to get behind!

Some years ago, a man with one child told me he could not sleep at night because he could not understand how I was doing well with so many children, while he had only one! The best thing he could have done for himself was to mind his own business. I was praying, while he could not sleep!

I was young and now I am old, yet I have never seen the righteous forsaken, nor his seed begging bread. We managed to own three homes in England. We faced the threat of eviction, and almost went bankrupt—but God never forsook us. Things didn't always go smoothly. If I've hurt anyone along the way, please forgive me. I am human. But there's always love in my heart. I never intend to hurt anyone.

At the time of writing, we've been married 65 years. When we celebrated our 60th anniversary, we received a signed certificate from the late Queen Elizabeth II.

I told my children, *"When I am gone, if anyone comes to say, 'I am your father's child', tell them to go to hell!"* (pardon my expression). Those before me went this route, but I just hate having children with more than one woman.

A young woman once called me a liar because I am a Jamaican. She assumed all Jamaican men have children with multiple women.

Some years ago, I was interviewed by an American man, and after noting that I looked young for my age, he asked for the secret. I told him, *"It is because I only have one wife, and my wife would not stand for me having affairs. She says she does not share this aspect of life with anyone else!"*

Throughout my journey, I have been surrounded by loving people. I thank all who have helped me along the way. I'm still in the batting crease—more rounds to go. You may have to put up with me for a while yet! One of my daughters told someone recently, *"My daddy is not going anywhere!"*

But if I do go before you, promise me that you will meet me on the other side. This is a beautiful world, but we've made a mess of it. Let's strive to enter sweet Beulah Land—the land of honey and sweet wine.

Heaven is better than this. If it were only in this life where we had hope, we would have been men most miserable. We have hope.

God is so, so good! I encourage you to serve God with all your heart. Put your trust in Him. He will never leave you nor forsake you.

As a child, my mother told me, *"If someone does you ninety-nine wrong deeds and one good deed, forget the ninety-nine wrong deeds and remember the one good deed."*

My father, a local farmer, inherited several parcels of land from his father. One was known as 'the Big Land.' He never brought home all the crops for himself. Others would always get something—bananas, breadfruit, ackee, potatoes... You name it!

What is in your hand? Use it. Be kind to others.

Chapter 6

All Aboard!

As first-time migrants who came to England to seek work, we did our best to get jobs on the British Rail, the Post Office or the London Underground and Buses.

I made several attempts to get a job on the buses, but they just would not employ me even though I passed all the tests. I mentioned earlier that I was good at mathematics and the tests for conductors was mostly about passing the maths test.

As the saying goes, *if at first you don't succeed, try and try again until you do*. I had been trying to get a job with London Transport since 1958, and I didn't get through until 1965.

I was happy when I finally got the job as a conductor. All my plans to return to Jamaica had gone out of the window. I was now married with children to support. At last, I had a secure job with a pension. This job demanded all that is within a man: honesty, fairness to all races, integrity, discipline and good character.

Before getting this job as a conductor, I had worked in Central London as a porter at a civic hall. One of my duties was to clean up rooms after meetings were rounded off. One Monday morning, I went to clean up a room where there had been music and dancing during the weekend. I was on my own in this room when I saw a cigarette box. When I opened it out of curiosity, I found £13.00 in this box - two weeks' wages for me at the time. Without hesitation, I handed it to the manager.

Months later, there was a petty session held in the larger hall by magistrates and JPs. On the side of the table where the magistrates sat, there was a £5 note left on the table. There was no one in this room, but I handed the money in.

Later, when I was offered the job on the buses, London Transport asked for references from my previous employers. I gave them the civic hall's address, and they wrote to the manager inquiring about my honesty.

I visited him afterwards, and he told me, *"London Transport wrote to me about you. I told them, 'One hundred percent.' Anyone who finds a five-pound note and hands it in is trustworthy."*

However, the job also required resilience. Just a few months into the job, I had an encounter with a black woman who tried to pay her fare using more coins than I was obligated to accept. When I told her so, she responded by cursing my wife and mother, two women she had never even met!

Once we got over Vauxhall Bridge, I'd had enough. I told her she would have to leave the bus due to her rude behaviour. She refused at first, but I said the bus would not move until she got off. I had the driver call for support, but she left before the police or an inspector arrived.

She later wrote a letter of complaint to London Transport about how I treated her. Surely, she didn't write it herself; the level of abuse she had hurled at me and my family spoke volumes about her ignorance and low self-esteem.

My manager read the letter and called me in. He began with, *"Mr. Hyatt, it appears you won't be a conductor much longer..."*

I was shocked. *"Excuse me, sir, can I tell you my side of the story?"*

I explained what had happened and how she had cursed my family. He was stunned and responded, *"Leave it with us. We will deal with it."*

Let me be clear, I wouldn't tolerate nonsense from anyone: black, white, pink, or yellow. I had a job to do, and I did it with fairness and integrity. Not even my wife or children travelled for free on a bus I was conducting. If you didn't have a valid pass or authority to travel, you paid. Simple.

There was no way I would allow anyone rude to travel on that bus. Sometimes a passenger would remark that it was not my bus, and I would reply, *"If it were my bus, you would not be allowed to travel on it!"*

"Wait. They will soon kick you off," they would retort.

"Yes, but I won't be coming to beg bread from you!" was my usual reply.

Some would threaten and say, *"Wait until I see you off this bus!"*

"When you see me off this bus, you would be too scared to come near me!" I was never intimidated.

Some young men would board a bus and refuse to pay their fares. They tried it with me, and I refused to accept their bad behaviour. After which, they would not attempt boarding a bus I was conducting.

It did not matter who you were; I did not allow anyone to be rude to me or do things that were unacceptable under the Road Traffic Act throughout my days working on the buses.

We were travelling up Hyde Park towards Marble Arch one day when a hot-tempered gentleman did something he should not have done. I called to him and told him what he did was wrong. His response was, *"Do you know who you are speaking to?"*

I retorted, *"I am talking to you, Sir. Who do you think you are?"*

His response was, *"I am going to report you."*

In return, I showed him my badge with my license number and added, *"Go ahead. Report me and tell London Transport what you have done."* I never heard from him again.

During the South African apartheid crisis, a white woman boarded at Oxford Street. She misbehaved, and I corrected her. She snapped, *"If you were in South Africa, you wouldn't even be allowed to conduct a bus!"* I replied, *"We'll be coming over there to kick you all out."* The whole bus erupted in laughter. A black girl joined in and gave her a proper dressing down.

It was a tough job working with the public, but thank God I survived!

I was once reported by a young white woman who was looking for trouble. One day she boarded the bus and left her baby push chair on the platform. I asked her to move it and she refused saying I should move it, but I said I would not!

She went home and reported me, claiming I was rude to her when she boarded the bus. I told my manager she always got on the bus seeking trouble. My manager tore up the letter and got the record book out.

By then, I had put in many years of service on the job. When he opened the book, his comments were, "Look at this! Only your name was written in the book. That's not good enough. Your address should also be written in the book.'

And that was all about it.

One day, I was called into the office about someone who reported me for something I had no recollection of. After the manager spoke to me, he said, *"Don't worry, Mr Hyatt. We know you are doing a good job out there."*

A white man once got on the bus and refused to pay his fare, saying he earned £100.00, and they took £20.00 for tax. I pointed out to him that everybody paid taxes, and he would have to pay his fare. He refused, and when he wanted to leave the bus, I refused to let him get off the bus until we reached the next stop, where inspectors would be on duty. He got physical, kicked me in the mouth, and I got hold of him. Everyone on the bus begged me not to kill him.

At the bus stop, inspectors were called, and he was taken into the garage while they waited for the police to come. He was arrested on five charges, including assault. The case was tried, and I heard he pleaded guilty and was fined £75.00, which was a lot of money then. A very foolish man he was!

In another situation, a black man got on the bus and did not pay the correct fare for where he was going. I went and informed him that the fare he paid would not take him any further. When he refused to pay more and insisted he was not getting off the bus, Central Control was informed of the situation.

Incidentally, around that time, four police outriders were passing by, and they were called to come over to handle the situation. In the presence of these police officers, this man started using abusive language towards me. The police surrounded him with their horses. He tried to leave, but they told him, *"No, you are not going anywhere. You are under arrest. Right in our presence, you abused the conductor. If you abused him, you abused us."* He was arrested and charged. On the day of the case, I was called to give evidence, and during the trial, he threatened me. He was found guilty and given a custodial sentence.

There is so much I could say about the things that happened while I was working on the buses!

In the late 1980s, young people began going to late night parties. A duty was started on our rota schedule for picking up passengers in Crystal Palace, South London.

No crew wanted to work this duty because these young men and women were very abusive and refused to pay their fares. It was so bad that our Union had to call for a strike on the matter. Then, at some point, I was assigned to work this duty.

It was a Saturday evening duty. My driver and I took the bus to Crystal Palace. When the passengers started to board the bus, these young people went upstairs and filled all the seats on the top deck.

I told my driver, *"When we get to the bus stop opposite the police station, don't move the bus until I tell you to do so."*

I then went upstairs to collect all fares, and no one wanted to pay their fare. Pointing to the police station, I announced to them, *"The bus will not move until all fares are paid. If not, I will call the police over there."*

At this point, everyone paid the correct fare to where they intended to alight!

When they were leaving the bus, they all came patting me on the shoulder, saying, *"You're cool, man. You are so cool!"* I replied, "Great! Go and enjoy yourselves". They were my children's age, so why should I be intimidated?

An African man once called me a slave for working on the buses. I responded, *"Yes. So were your forefathers who sold their people into slavery."* The bus roared with laughter.

There was this white woman who boarded the bus with her dog without asking permission, as the rules required her to do. To make matters worse, she put the dog on the seat, which was not allowed in any case. I asked her to take the dog off the seat, and she refused, adding that her dog was cleaner than me!

This statement was like waving a red flag to a bull. I told her she had to leave the bus, but she refused. The police were called to get her off the bus.

A black man also did the same thing, and when I asked him to take the dog off the seat, he told me to 'F' off. Again, the police were called to get him off the bus.

One day, while I was conducting the bus, a young woman told me, *"I would love to have you for a husband."*

"How do you know we would get on?" I asked.

"We would get on because I always travel on your bus and I see how you conduct the bus..." She also added, *"If your wife puts up with you, so will I."*

I invited her to come to church with me, that she might find a man to love. But she declined the invitation, saying that if she attended my church, her eyes would only be on me!

At least she was honest. Why go to church with someone you love but can't have in your life? What she did not understand was that seeing a man and living with him are two different things. How was she sure we would get on together? "Don't buy puss in a bag," as Jamaicans would say.

When I joined London Transport, I was paired with a white English driver. We got along so well that he brought my wife home from the hospital after childbirth and came to our children's christenings. We were even interviewed by ITV about our friendship during a time of workplace discrimination reform.

I did not see him just as a white man. As a Jamaican, I knew of the things our ancestors went through. My father was brought up by a white family in Jamaica. Some of our grandparents were white. I have two beautiful mixed-race granddaughters from our son.

We, as black people, ought to be proud of ourselves. They wanted to throw us out, but we are going nowhere. Instead, we brought flavour to this country! When we came here, you could only get fish and chips wrapped in newspaper, roast potatoes with beef stew, half-down steak, sausage and cheese, bacon and chips.

My bus driver used to complain that he was fed up with sausage and chips, bacon, egg and chips. Meanwhile, I was going home to eat roast chicken, rice and peas, curried goat and roast potatoes, and sometimes fresh fish - and don't forget ackee and salt-fish. Mr. Churchill used to love this dish when he was alive and visited Jamaica.

We did have black cooks in the staff canteen at London Transport, and the time came when rice and peas were added to the menu. Our white colleagues first frowned at the idea, but after a while, they started to order it.

We truly brought flavour to this country!

I am now going to advertise my sweet, sweet Jamaica!

Take a holiday trip to this sunny country. Book yourself into a four-star hotel. Sit back and relax, brother. Maybe you may not want to come back to your fish and chips!

You may ask, *"If it was so good in Jamaica, why did you come to this cold country?"* My answer would be, *"We came to give you flavour! Mi com man, mi nuh go nowhere."*

In early 1992, we were informed that London Transport Buses would start running as a one-man operation. This was a shock for us as conductors, as many of us were near pension age. Some of us still had mortgages to pay. How were we going to manage?

A London Transport Director was sent to tell us what was going to happen, and also about the redundancy package that would be offered. I asked him, *"Why are we being treated in this manner after years of faithful service?"*

He looked me up in the records and said, *"Mr. Hyatt, you have a very good record. Not even I have such a good record. If you don't want to go, we will find you a job."*

I was now nearing retirement, so I reluctantly accepted early retirement. Life was not going to be easy, but I trusted in God.

"Trust in the Lord with all your heart... Acknowledge him and he will direct thy path."
Proverbs 3:5-6

After accepting redundancy, I got a debt collection job. It was tough. My duty was to go and see clients who were in debt and were unable to meet their obligations.

I remember going to see a woman who owed £8,000. She was single. After we agreed on the amount she would be able to pay, I asked her, *"How come you got yourself into this situation?"* From what she shared, she had a boyfriend on whose behalf she had borrowed money so she could help him. Unfortunately, he walked out of her life.

Hearing things like this made my blood boil.

Come on, men! How would you like someone to treat your mother, sister or aunt in such a dishonest manner? Be a man and stand up to your responsibilities! Someone borrowed money, helped him, and he walked away without repaying? He should have been charged with theft, tried and put in jail with hard labour!

Someone loaned me £5,000 and wanted to write the debt off. But I declined the offer. I told him I would make arrangements for it to be repaid. God did help me to clear that debt.

Even as I worked, my desire for further education was always there. I decided to get enrolled in college to study Maths and English. My tutor was not always available, but I got the Maths book, looked at it and kept getting all my answers right.

About this time, the news reached me that my mother had passed away in Jamaica, so I had to travel to attend her funeral. I spent over four weeks on the Island and then returned to the College to complete my studies in readiness for the exams.

My tutor was so impressed at how I was getting my maths right even when I was not around, that she decided to put me forward to take my exams. I did it and passed my City and Guild examination at the age of 65!

I also worked as an Insurance Consultant for five years, after which I got a job as a Security officer.

Almost all through my working years, I was continually under pressure from women who wanted me to either date them or marry them, regardless of their age or status. Now, after retirement and working as a Security Officer, it started all over again. This time, it got ridiculous.

I went to work on a site outside London, and a young black lady was working in the office. She told me she was a Christian and was glad to communicate, so we used to sit together in the restaurant. All the other workers were non-Christians, and every other word was a swear word, so it was refreshing to have a Christian to talk to.

One day, we sat around the table and were talking. During the conversation, I would often mention my wife, and to my utmost surprise, she got upset that I kept mentioning my wife. After that day, I tried to keep a distance, but it did not matter where I was posted; she would find me.

I got posted back to London, and she moved to London as well, calling to inform me that she was looking for a flat and as soon as she found one, she would be inviting me over. After she got the flat, she called, asking me to come and visit her. She had my phone number because I was going to invite her to a planned birthday party.

After telling my wife about it, I told her I would not be coming to visit her, which upset her a great deal. A while later, she called again to let me know she was now married. I congratulated her and wished her well.

Not long after that, she phoned to let me know she now had a baby and wanted me to see the child. I have not heard from her since. I was not going to put myself into a situation where things could go wrong. I am a man of God, a licensed minister of religion.

"Let your light so shine before men that they may see your good works and glorify your Father in heaven."

(Matthew 5:16)

After my wife and I got married, we settled down in the Church of God of Prophecy, where we have worshipped and served faithfully over the years.

At some point, our deacon was not in good health, and he recommended that I be put forward as the next deacon. It was the policy of the church that anyone seeking this office should have some background in Biblical training.

The church was operating three years of Biblical Studies, so I enrolled and, by God's grace, passed all three courses. Upon concluding these courses, you are given a certificate for each year's study. This was close to thirty-five years ago.

Eventually, I was ordained and licensed a Deacon at the annual convention of the Church of God of Prophecy, United Kingdom. The church has its Head office in Birmingham, while the worldwide office is in the U.S.A.

I did not stop there. I also furthered my Biblical knowledge by studying all sixty-six books of the Bible.

Chapter 7

TEMPTATIONS AND DELIVERANCE

I believe this aspect of my story is worth sharing, as it may help others walk carefully and make wise decisions.

Growing up, I was not a saint. Severally, I found myself involved in situations that caused grief. Up until I was 14 years old, girls were willing to engage with me, and they were often the instigators. I recall being caught by my mother with a girl in the outside toilet, and she chastised me. I was also caught in a toilet by the girl's father, who spanked her and informed my father of the incident, leading to my own punishment.

Thankfully, things began to change for me between the ages of 15 and 16. I was no longer allowed to associate with anyone, male or female, without good reason, and I was required to be indoors after 6 pm. I also had to attend Sunday school each week. after I also gave my heart to the Lord at the age of 17. All these helped to mould me into a respectable young person.

My mentor, Esmine Cottrel, played a crucial role in my spiritual development. She was about four years older than I and had taken me to Sunday school since I was three. Her guidance was instrumental in earning the respect of both young and old in the district.

As I continued to grow in my faith, my life transformed significantly. The changes were evident to those around me. On one occasion, while walking along our local road, a man was cursing all the young men in the area. Upon seeing me, he remarked, *"Not you, young man! You can enter any home in the district and ask for their daughter, and you would be accepted."*

After I moved to Kingston, a young girl from my district began communicating with me. We fell in love and started writing to each other. When I visited America, I showed my friends one of her letters. A man who saw it remarked, *"You must marry this girl!"*

Upon my return to Jamaica, I bought some clothing for the girl I had been dating. One day, her mother approached me during a walk in the district.

"I saw you bought things for my daughter. Do you love her?" She inquired.

"I do, and will be coming to see you about her..." I assured her.

This woman spoke highly of me to my father, praising my gentlemanly behaviour when she approached me. She expressed that I was the only young man in the district she wanted as her son-in-law.

Around this time, I decided to travel to England. Just before I left, I visited her home on a Sunday to seek her permission to marry her daughter. She was delighted and reiterated, *"You are the only young man in the district I would gladly agree for my daughter to marry."*

The girl's father had passed away when she was young, leaving behind two houses for his daughters.

I waited for this young girl to come and meet me at her mother's home. When she arrived, she showed no interest in marrying me. Her mother became distressed and began to cry, stating that her daughter did not love her; otherwise, she would agree to marry me.

The girl's older sister, a teacher, became furious upon learning of the situation and threatened to disinherit her from their father's estate.

Eventually, she confided in me about her reluctance to marry. She was only 17 and wished to pursue a profession before entering marriage. I promised her that I would wait five years before we married, as I too wanted to establish my career.

As I previously mentioned, despite the attention I received from many young women, I remained focused. I believed that all young Christians should wait on God to provide a life partner, as not everyone is meant to be a life partner.

While I was pursued by women, I was not interested in anyone other than my future wife. One young woman, unhappy that I did not propose to her, was furious when I eventually got married. I invited her to visit us, but she refused.

It would have been madness for me to marry someone I did not love. I trusted that in time, she would find someone who loved her in return.

In the early days of my marriage, a young man asked me, *"If you met a beautiful young woman who loved you more than your wife, what would you do?"*

The question struck me as strange, given that he was my wife's cousin. I replied, *"I wouldn't do anything because I am already married."*

Later, I learned that he was seeking my opinion because he was in such a situation himself.

Young men, do not be fooled! The charmer you see now could bring disaster later on.

While working on the buses, I met a young man who was a driver. He was married, but he left his wife for another young woman. He later told me how he and this other woman bought a house, and as soon as they did, she threw him out of the house! He attempted to return to his wife, but she would not have him back. He regretted leaving his beautiful wife for this woman. What did he expect? Be satisfied with what you have.

Throughout my marriage, I have faced my share of unwanted attention from women, including some who were married.

One married woman, who claimed to be a Christian, invited me to stay overnight while her husband was on night shift. When I visited her for business, she pretended to be sick and lay in bed, clearly attempting to seduce me. When I informed my wife, she felt the woman was being very disrespectful, wanting to put me in a compromising position.

There were also married women who, upon my visits to congratulate them on their new babies, would claim that the child should have been mine!

It was the same even during my visits to Jamaica. I maintained my boundaries, stating, *"No, I can't, because I am married and I am also a Christian."*

Before my marriage, while working at an old people's home, I encountered a married woman who sought me out wherever I was assigned. I resisted her advances, unaware that she was married and lived in the home of my future wife's father.

While she was attempting to seduce me, she was going home, telling the young woman who was to be my future wife about me, and how handsome I was, and she should try meeting up with me.

This world is indeed small, my friends. Be cautious in your actions and words; someone is always watching. We live in an uncertain world, so walk carefully, for danger may be near. You could find yourself facing a test that could haunt you.

A young Christian woman came up from Jamaica to study nursing. She married a man from a smaller island, but unfortunately backslid in her faith. She confided that her parents had forsaken her. One day, she cornered me, expressing her love for me. I looked her in the eye and firmly stated, *"There is a gulf between us; you are married, and I am a Christian. It will not work!"*

She released me but continued to hope I would change my mind. Later, she informed me that she had separated from her husband.

When I first came to England, a young woman was living in the same building as I was. She was pregnant, but I never saw the man responsible.

She was young and beautiful, around 19 years old, and I initially believed her husband had a good job. I later discovered she was involved with a man in Jamaica who married someone else but sent for her, getting her pregnant while still living with his wife.

Some men can be truly evil! He brought this young woman to a foreign country, got her pregnant, and abandoned her! How someone could be so cruel is beyond me.

This young woman always showed a likeness for me. She moved from the house we were all living in and told my brother she was in love with me and wanted to marry me. When my brother told her I would not marry her because she had a child, she sent the child to her mother in Jamaica to get the child out of the way.

My brother, knowing I was a Christian, arranged for her to visit me alone to tempt me. She later spread false rumours that I had impregnated her, threatening to kill me with a knife.

News of these accusations reached Jamaica, causing the girl I had promised to marry to refuse to come over for our wedding.

There was another young woman I wrote to, inviting her to marry me, but she, too, declined to move to England. Years later, when she migrated, I was already married. I later learned she was in an asylum. According to her sister, she ended up in an asylum after visiting us and realising what she had missed out on.

Years later, she expressed her regrets for not marrying me, which drove her to madness. When I collected something my father had given her to pass on to me, her behaviour was strange, as she hurriedly asked me to leave her house.

She confided in me about her life struggles, expressing her regret about not marrying me. She wanted us to meet at her workplace, but I declined, believing that prevention is better than cure.

My wife once asked me, "Do you still love her?" I replied, "Yes, I do love her, but she was not the woman God intended for me!" I cannot forget how I prayed for a wife and the dreams I had of my future partner.

Another young woman had expressed her desire to get married to me. Her mother had told her that she only wanted me as her son-in-law – no one else. When she learned of my impending marriage, she travelled to England with the intention of stopping the wedding, but she was told that it was too late. She became regretful of not marrying me, and nearly went crazy.

Let God's will be done in your life, my friends, whether young or old. The Israelites desired a king, just like everyone else, and we see the consequences of that decision. Let God's will be your will.

While Jesus Christ was in the garden praying, we are told He made this cry to His father: *"If it be possible, let this cup pass from me; nevertheless, not my will but yours"*.

If His son, who knew no sin, was willing to do His Father's will, what about you and me, wretched sinners, who are unworthy of living on the beautiful earth God has created?

While walking in Croydon Town, a woman I did not know approached me, saying, *"Take me for your girlfriend."* I replied, *"No, my wife would not like that."* Her friend chimed in, *"You don't have to tell your wife."*

"Guide me, oh thou great redeemer, pilgrim
through this barren land;
I am weak, but thou art strong, hold me
with your powerful hands."

If you profess to be a Christian, let your light shine. You cannot do it alone; you are no match for Satan, who comes to kill and destroy.

He tried it with our Lord Jesus Christ, but Jesus told him, *"Get behind me, Satan."* Never allow him to stand in front of you; he offers nothing but sin, shame, and disgrace.

I was on a plane returning from Jamaica after visiting my parents, who were still alive. A white man sat opposite me and seemed determined to provoke me.

The stewardess noticed his behaviour and offered to move me, but I refused to be intimidated. We were all paying passengers; why should I move?

Unbeknownst to me, this was a plot of the devil to lead me astray! Keep your eyes on Jesus even when you are some 35,000 miles up in the air!

We were served hot drinks, and this man suddenly jerked my table, causing me to spill hot liquid on myself. I drew the attention of the stewardess and requested to be moved, wishing to avoid any trouble on the plane.

The stewardess relocated me to a window seat with two empty seats beside me. I wore a tailored suit, and when a young white girl sat by the window, she hurriedly went to the toilet and stayed there for an extended period.

I wondered if she disliked black people and asked to change seats. When she finally returned to her seat, she asked for my assistance in filling out a migration form, as she was visiting London for a holiday.

She moved closer to me, professing interest, going so far as to mention that she had previously dated a black man and knew how to cook for black people.

She told me the hotel she was staying at and how she did not have anyone to take her around London. From her actions, she was prepared to die in my arms if the plane were to crash. She was an American and very beautiful.

After the plane landed, I had to wait over four hours to clear immigration, and she stayed with me the entire time. When my eldest daughter came to meet me, I noticed her expression change dramatically.

There was no way I was going to sacrifice my salvation and marriage for this or any other woman, regardless of their affections. I had been taken in by a woman who understood her desires!

I have made it my motto never to deceive a woman; my word is my bond. I have witnessed men claiming to love a woman while lying. My mother raised me to speak the truth and nothing but the truth. Those who hide their actions are still doing wrong!

It would be very difficult for me to go to court and not speak the truth.

I once had a car due for an MOT (Ministry of Transport Test). Overnight, someone damaged it badly. It was also due for tax, and someone reported it to the GLC, leading to a court summons.

Someone said I should get a lawyer, and I said, *"What for?"* On the day of the court hearing, the case was called up. I stood in the dock, with a man standing by my side, ready to take me to jail, I assumed.

When asked how I wished to plead, I replied, *"Guilty, my Lord, with explanation!"* I explained why my car was unlicensed and how I had only £1 to buy a cup of tea while it was being towed away.

The magistrates were shocked by my account and sympathised with me. One magistrate instructed the man beside me to step away.

She then declared, *"We are going to discharge the case against you, but you will have to pay the tax now due."* Relieved, I put my hand in my pocket and pulled out my wallet, ready to pay the car tax, but was told I would have to go downstairs and pay at the cashier.

Why should I get a lawyer when I am an untrained lawyer myself? I wish I had studied law!

A beautiful young woman once asked if I would have affairs. When I replied, *"No! I am married and I am a Christian,"* she reminded me that Christians do have affairs.

While I have heard of such cases, I urge anyone reading this: stop engaging in sinful acts. A day will come when you must account for your deeds!

As treasurer of our church, we were expected to produce annual accounts to our head office. I once discovered an untraceable expenditure, which frustrated me greatly. I persisted until I discovered it was a motor tax payment. A tax inspector reviewed our books and praised my accounting practices.

Good accounting is essential, my brothers and sisters. You will stand before God at the Judgment Seat, and what will your response be? The angels are recording everything, and they will make no mistakes. What will you say?

Let me share a true story from about 80 years ago. A man owned two shops. His wife managed one while he managed the other in a different area within the same district. He visited another area and became involved with a younger woman. He got so intoxicated with the affair to the point of scheming to get rid of the wife. He planned to invite the wife to the girlfriend's home for dinner and poison her so they could live together.

The man fell ill that Thursday, died on Friday, and was buried on Sunday. It was his girlfriend who confessed to their plan at his funeral. Our home was opposite his shop, and I still bear a scar on my left knee from an accident that occurred on that same day.

Men, for heaven's sake, do not play with your Maker! He will not allow you to escape your wrongdoings, regardless of your race. Be warned; the bearers are waiting at the door!

Let me share with you some more incredible stories of some young women that may shock you.

As previously mentioned, when I began working as a security officer, I was assigned to a college in London. Shortly after my arrival, a young girl approached my desk and boldly stated, "Make me one of your girlfriends." I replied, "No, I can't. I am married and I am a Christian." She walked away without further comment. A few weeks later, she returned.

"Make me one of your wives. I am a Muslim, and Muslims have more than one wife", she said.

Once again, I responded as before. Two weeks later, I asked her age, and she revealed she was 18.

I was taken aback and tried to encourage her, *"You are young. Finish your studies. Find a young man who will marry you and don't allow any man to use you"*.

An 18-year-old girl requesting an affair with a 64-year-old man! What does this generation seek? At 18, I was eager to reach 21!

An Eastern-looking young girl also approached me, strikingly beautiful and with an alluring figure. I once inquired why she wore revealing clothes, and she replied that it was her preference.

Once, she missed her class and stayed at my desk for over four hours. When her mates asked her why she wouldn't leave me alone, she responded, *"He is nice, I love him"*, or words to that effect.

She turned to me one day and said, *"Ron, the best thing that could happen to me next year is to get pregnant"*.

"Why do you want to get pregnant?" I asked.

"I want to have children. I love children," she replied.

"Why don't you finish your studies, start your career, find a young man to marry you, then start having children?" I queried her.

"I don't want them," she retorted.

"I am too old for that," I said, with a smile on my face.

"You are not too old," she insisted, but I did not bulge or give in.

For God's sake, please make the right choices!

Shortly after that encounter, I was reassigned to a Borough Council Office, where temptations persisted. This time, a beautiful young Portuguese woman approached me, expressing the same desire to be my girlfriend. Again, I responded, *"No, I am married, and I am a minister. I cannot hurt you or my wife."*

One day, she came and asked to see my ring. She accused me of lying, but I insisted, stating the exact number of years I had been married. She just would not stop asking questions. Another time, she came up to my desk and announced, *"I want you to find me a husband."*

I empathise with this generation, as there seem to be insufficient responsible young men willing to commit. All they desire is a fleeting encounter, moving on to the next victim.

These young women seek security, believing that older generations can fulfil that need in their lives.

As Christians, we must encourage our young people, reminding them that there is another way. God can provide for all our needs. If you have read this far, you will see there is a way out. No government can provide everything we need in this life, but Jesus can. He understands all our pains and struggles, so do not let them overwhelm you. There is hope, my dear friend. Yes, there is hope!

Soon, I will be ending with an invitation for you to look into your life and decide to seek God before it is too late. Jesus is coming soon.

Top left: Our first son and first daughter. **Top right:** Rita and I, on our wedding day. **Bottom left:** Rita and I, and Rita's father. **Bottom right:** Rita and I on our 50th wedding anniversary.

Top left: Rita and I at a wedding ceremony. **Top right:** Rita and I, cutting our wedding cake. **Bottom left:** Youthful Rita before we got married. **Bottom right:** Rita and I with our first son.

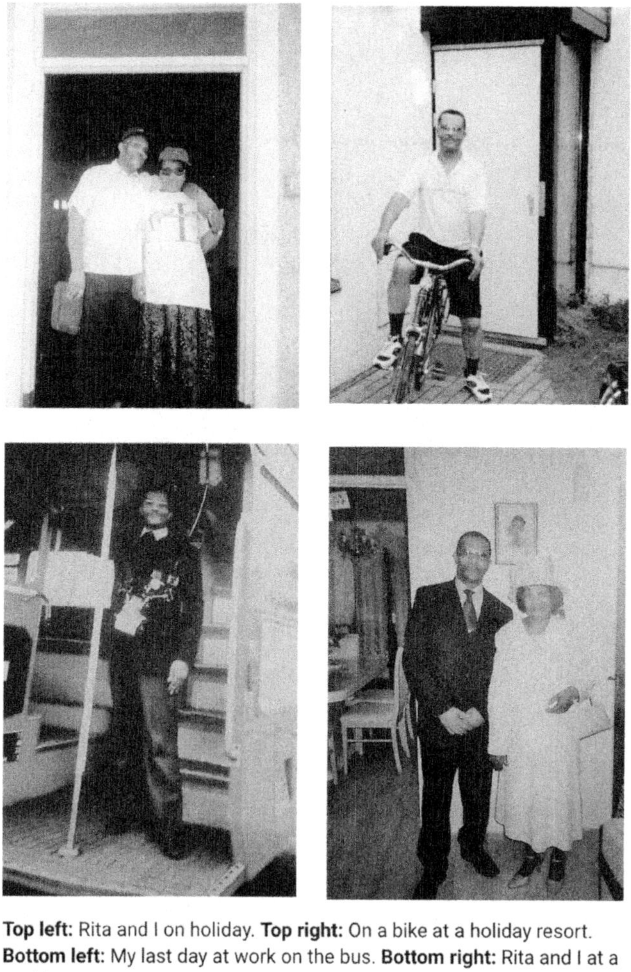

Top left: Rita and I on holiday. **Top right:** On a bike at a holiday resort. **Bottom left:** My last day at work on the bus. **Bottom right:** Rita and I at a wedding.

Top left: My 90th birthday. **Top right:** Rita and I. In the background, Her Majesty the late queen Elizabeth II, who gave us a congratulation certificate for our 60th anniversary. **Bottom left:** Rita and I on holiday. **Bottom right:** My 90th birthday.

Top: (From left) My mother, Rita's mother, and my father.
Bottom: Rita and I at our grandson's wedding.

Top left: Rita and I at a wedding. **Top right:** At a church. **Bottom left:** Rita and I on holiday in Jamaica. **Bottom right:** Rita's birthday.

Top: Our 50th Wedding Anniversary. **Bottom:** Our children (inset: our youngest child).

CHAPTER 8

MIRACLES AND TESTIMONIES

My dear friends, God is real. He will answer your prayers if you approach Him sincerely. My life is filled with testimonies of answered prayers and God's constant supernatural interventions.

My wife was once severely ill with rheumatoid arthritis, struggling to walk and reliant on a walking stick. The doctors recommended surgery, but we refused, choosing instead to pray for her healing and trust in the Lord. Her mother, a devoted believer serving God in Jamaica, was also praying for her.

We were advised to consult an *Obia* man, as it was suggested that the girl whose mother insisted she wanted no other son-in-law but me was somehow behind my wife's condition. I dismissed this as nonsense; I knew both the mother and her daughter from our district, and I could not believe they would resort to such actions.

One day, our pastor and two other Christian brethren visited while I was at work and prayed for my wife. Miraculously, she was healed!

On another occasion, my wife fell ill again, and the doctors were baffled by her condition. I took her to see a private doctor, who examined her and insisted she needed to be admitted to the hospital for an operation. I returned to our family doctor, who reluctantly agreed and arranged for an ambulance to take her.

Upon arrival at the hospital, a female doctor informed me that we were fortunate; if my wife had not been admitted, she would have been dead within 24 hours.

When we were expecting our fifth child, my wife became gravely ill, prompting our doctor to refer her to a consultant. The consultant advised that an abortion was necessary, as there was no way she could give birth without complications.

My wife firmly replied that we would not agree to abort the baby, as we were Christians and believed God would help her deliver safely.

When the time for the birth arrived, I informed the hospital that my wife was in labour. They instructed me to call for an ambulance to take her in, as they prepared the operating theatre.

Upon arriving at the hospital, she gave birth to a healthy baby girl within ten minutes. That same baby girl has since grown into a healthy young woman and now works as a manager in the NHS!

Yes, our God does answer prayers! He comes to our aid when we face serious problems. If we are thrown into the fire, He will be right there with us! When unjustly imprisoned, He can send thunder and earthquakes to blast down the prison doors! He is the living God!

Earlier, I mentioned how I was made redundant from a job I had held for 28 years. We had a mortgage, but we fell behind on our payments.

The mortgage lender decided to take us to court to repossess our home. A relative loaned us part of the arrears, and the Citizens' Advice Bureau contacted the lender to inform them of our partial payment and request the withdrawal of the court case.

They refused, insisting on taking the house away from us.

A church sister, a widow, learned of our situation and felt compelled to help. She offered us her bank book to withdraw all her savings to pay off the mortgage arrears! We declined her generous offer, stating we could only withdraw what was necessary, as a relative had already lent us part of the money.

On the day of the court trial, a representative from the lender called us into a room to explain the proceedings. We informed him that we had managed to gather all the arrears. He was astonished and agreed to call off the repossession case.

Just a few years later, we sold our house and purchased another outright with cash!

Oh, how I love Jesus!

I have a home built for me in heaven, mortgage-free and rent-free. I will not have to worry about payments because the blood of Jesus has paid that mortgage loan! If you were offered such a wonderful deal in this world, what would you do? Jesus said He has gone to prepare a place for us and will return to take us to His Father.

Come on, friend. Embrace this offer without delay! It will not last forever. He is coming soon, and only those who are faithful and accept this offer will see the Father, who is also our Father. Please do not waste any more of your precious time. Seek the Lord before it is too late. Heaven's door will soon be shut, and when it is, where will you go? There are only two places: heaven or hell. Choose wisely.

You have been warned: there will be no excuses for not having heard that Jesus died for your sins and that He will return for His own if you repent and serve Him faithfully. Tell your family and friends that you have read this book, and encourage them to get their copies and read carefully.

There have also been times when I was weak.

I experienced a period of spiritual weakness some years ago. Things were not going right; I was in debt and without a job to support myself and my family. I went on a ten-day fast. At a point, I lay stretched out, held my breath and told God, *"If you can't change things, take me out of this world now"*.

It was after these ten days of fasting that I secured a job as a security officer. God knew I would face many temptations, and He led me into ten days of fasting, drawing me closer to Him. That is why I was able to resist sin.

Get closer to God, my friends. He gives power to the faint and strengthens those who are weak. As the hymn writer wrote, *"I am weak, but Thou art mighty; hold me with Your powerful hands."*

I love the people and the songs we sing here, but heaven is far better than this. That is why I have promised to serve God as long as He gives me breath. I have come too far to look back now, and I will follow Him until the day I die.

"Goodbye, world, I am gone.

Goodbye, world, I am on my way to heaven.

And I won't go back from whence I came."

The journey is not easy, but with Him by my side, I can face tomorrow.

"Spirit of the living God, fall afresh on me, mould me, cleanse me, fill me, fall afresh on me".

"I've got my mind made up and I won't turn back. I am on my way to heaven, and I won't turn back, glory hallelujah; I am on my way to heaven, and I won't turn back!!"

Have you laid your all on the altar yet? You will only be blessed and find sweet peace when all is laid on the altar. Will your anchor hold when the stormy clouds rage? Only you can answer these questions.

We have an anchor that keeps the soul firmly grounded in the Saviour's arm.

May the blessings of God be with you and comfort you in the name of Jesus Christ, His Son.

Chapter 9

A Burden and a Prayer

My 90 years on this earth have been full of joy, family bereavements, sadness, having more than what I need, and sometimes not having enough. Sometimes I had money in my pockets, other times I would wonder where the next pence would come from.

In my first job in the UK, my pay packet was £7.10 shillings per week. By the time I decided to retire at 69 years old, my salary had grown to over £21,000 per year. However, money is not everything. Health and happiness come first, and above all, God should always be placed first in your life.

My mother did her best to give me three types of garments to wear. First was the Sunday best. This outfit was reserved for Sundays or special church functions. Woe betides you if you returned home from church and failed to change into your everyday clothes;

they were referred to as your 'judging clothes'. I also had what was called 'special second dressing clothes'. This attire was for outings to town or other interesting places. Then, of course, play garments.

I went hungry many times, yet I was content with what little I had, whether great or small, remaining joyful and hopeful for better times ahead. I was raised not to covet what others possessed. With all our earthly wealth, we cannot take anything with us. Besides, Satan does not desire your money; he wants your soul.

I once heard a story about a rich man with two sons. He instructed them that when he died, they should place all his cash into his casket. Upon his death, the older son wrote a cheque for the entire amount.

The younger son, confused, turned to his brother and said, "Dad wanted all his money in cash!" The older brother replied, "Where do you think I can get that cash? I wrote him a cheque; let him cash it wherever he has gone!"

A poor man, left with only one ripe banana, decided to eat it and then end his life. He climbed a tree, placed a noose around his neck, peeled the banana, and dropped the skin on the ground.

Almost immediately, another man came along, picked up the banana skin, and began to eat it hungrily.

The man who had dropped the skin was alarmed. *"If there is someone worse off than me, then I will not kill myself."*

There will always be someone worse off than you, my friend, in your town, district, city, or across the globe.

Do not let the problems of this world bring you down. Others have faced greater hardships than you, both in the past and today. Each day, give thanks to God for sparing your life to see a brand-new day.

We were not wealthy, but my mother did everything in her power to ensure we had something to eat and clothes to wear. She was an excellent cook and dressmaker. However, she had an uncle in the district who was well-off, owning many acres of land and a large duplex, often employing four servants in my childhood.

During mealtimes, if the bell rang, it signalled that you should leave, as you would not be invited to sit at the large dining table unless you were a guest of high standing.

When he was still alive, I visited him in Jamaica. He lamented about all he had lost and how those he had helped were now better off than him. The large house had deteriorated to the point where you would be fortunate to see a single stone of its foundation.

He once stood for a local election and made a speech stating, "Who is up, stay up; and who is down, stay down." Those words sealed his fate. Everyone who had once supported him withdrew their backing and rallied around a less affluent candidate, who ultimately won the election. Whatever you have, be kind to others. Do not treat others anyhow.

This is a very dangerous world. Even those related to you might seek to bring you down. Think of the story of Joseph in the Bible; it was his brothers who betrayed him out of jealousy. The one they sought to demean later became the one who saved them.

The person you try to push aside today could be the one who may have to pull you out of the gutter tomorrow. Remember the Word of God: 'Do my servants no harm.'

During my childhood, there was a judge living in another area of our district who sometimes dressed so casually that it was hard to believe he was a judge. One day, while on his way to court, he offered a lift to a man who was walking. The man revealed he was on his way to court.

Unbeknownst to him, the man who had given him a lift was the judge who would try his case. The man, unaware of his audience, explained that he had been summoned for uttering bad words that he insisted he did not use.

In those days, certain swear words could lead to fines or imprisonment. A particular indecent word could earn a fine of forty shillings. Old-time Jamaicans know that word.

This man, unaware he was speaking to the judge, inadvertently sealed his fate by revealing too much. Upon entering the courtroom and seeing the judge, he fled in panic. The officers pursued him, but the judge instructed them to let him go and to serve him a fresh summons.

On the new trial date, the judge explained what had transpired and why the man had fled. He believed the man did not use the offensive words, and the case was dismissed.

Your words can determine your fate and future. Watch what you say and how you relate to others.

You may have heard of a woman in Jamaica who lived to be over one hundred and seventeen years old. I knew her well, as she lived on the same road as my father, and I often passed her house on my way to school or church. During one of my visits to the island, I stopped by to see her.

With her Bible open in front of her, she shared that she had just read about Moses living for one hundred and twenty years and hoped to do the same. At that time, she was a hundred and ten years old. She almost made it!

Life is too short to harbour hate and malice in our hearts. We are children of the living God; treat others with love. I recall something my mother told me during my childhood: if someone hurts you ninety-nine times but does one good deed, forget the ninety-nine bad deeds and remember that one good deed.

Our land spaces might be very large, but in fact, we are living in a very small world.

When I lived and worked in the United States, we were accommodated in a camp. Whenever our clothes became dirty, we would wash them and hang them out to dry. Being the youngest in the group, I set up a line to dry my clothes in the sun.

However, an older man took over all the hanging space. I informed him that I had put up the line and needed to hang my clothes. His reaction was to hurl insults and threaten to fight me. I calmly told him I would prefer to bury myself in the ground than engage in conflict with him.

I chose not to go to work that day. When the other men returned from work and heard what happened, they were furious and wanted to confront him, feeling protective of me as the youngest.

After we returned to Jamaica, I was waiting for my uncle's vehicle to take me back to my district to see my family. While on a street in Kingston called Parade, guess who turned up? It was the same guy who had taken over my clothesline in America. There were three other guys with him.

As soon as he saw me, he walked up to me with his friends and told them we had been in America together, and that I was a good Christian.

They stood guard over me until my uncle arrived to take me to the country. Had I chosen to fight this man in America, they could have dealt with me in Kingston, and I would not have stood a chance.

Christians, walk carefully. You never know what you will face. Put on the whole armour of God. Be wise as a serpent, and harmless as a dove!

Many years ago, someone told me that the reason I faced so many problems in life was that God wanted me to help others during their predicaments.

This world is indeed strange. Do not concern yourself with how others are faring. You cannot know how someone appears to have everything while you have nothing. How they acquired their wealth could be illegal. Do you wish to follow suit?

Whatever you might be going through, be honest and true to yourself and to others. You can't go wrong that way.

This is going to be a warning, not financial advice, even though I have had some training in the financial sector.

I understand how the financial system operates in terms of investments and insurance. After leaving the London Transport establishment, I became a financial adviser. There are things I knew then that I wish I had known before.

This is some fatherly advice, particularly for the younger generation.

Be very cautious regarding borrowing money. The banks are profit-driven. If you have a good credit score, as I did some years ago, they are quick to offer you a loan. However, if you fall behind on payments, you will find yourself alone.

They were quick to extend credit card limits, but once I missed payments, I was left stranded. It became so dire that I was advised to file for bankruptcy. I refused, insisting that God would help me clear my debts—and He did.

Watch your spending. Always set aside ten percent of your income and save it in a good savings account. When I came to England and began working, I ensured I had enough money to last until the next payday.

Be discerning with your purchases. It is better to invest in quality items that will endure than to buy cheap alternatives that require frequent replacement. I bought some of my outfits years ago, and they have served me well—well worth the price I paid for them.

Faithfulness to God is also essential. When I became a born-again Christian, I had few clothes or shoes to wear to church, but God opened doors for me. I now have many garments and footwear. Reflecting on this, I felt a voice speak to my heart: *"Because you were faithful to God, He is now rewarding you."*

When my church was purchasing a building, my wife and I often emptied our bank account to contribute to the mortgage needed to buy it. God rewarded us abundantly in many ways.

Do not be stingy with your money or resources. Give willingly and in love. Whatever seed you sow today, you will reap later. Seek to bear good fruit.

Several years ago, my father planted a tree that looked healthy, yet despite his efforts with fertiliser, it bore no fruit. Eventually, he cut it down. The axe is laid at the root of the tree to cut it down if it fails to be productive.

Seek the Lord while He may be found. Do not let the opportunity pass you by today, for tomorrow could be too late.

When I was about sixteen years old, I had an accident that resulted in four weeks in the hospital. There was an elderly man in the next bed who repeatedly said, *"Tell him to look under the tree..."* He kept repeating this phrase.

Both the doctors and nurses knew he was nearing death, and some stayed by his bedside, hoping to witness his last breath. I, too, was waiting to see when he would pass away. After we all stopped looking, a nurse came in, checked on him, and announced that he was gone. I was disappointed; I had been so close to him, but had not seen when he breathed his last.

I wonder what he had under that tree.

As children, we were told that in days gone by, when there were no banks, people would hide their money under trees. When they died, their relatives would dream of them, instructing them to look in a specific place for something.

Do not wait until it is too late to give your life to the true and living God.

I was told that when my father took ill, some of his church members went to visit him. After praying with him, a church brother promised, *"I am coming to visit you tomorrow"*.

My father replied, *"Don't come and visit me tomorrow. I won't be here. I am going home."* Just after midnight, he passed away to be with his Maker.

Knowing that you will leave this dark world for a better life is reassuring, but what about sudden death? A man may wake up fit and strong, with a good job and a lovely home, expecting to return after a day's work, only for news to break that he had an accident and died.

That's how life plays out sometimes, and it's all because of sin.

Blame Adam!

Take care of yourself. If you are not worshipping the true God, seek to do so now. You only have one life, and you will not return once it expires. For the child of God, they will enter a new world: no sickness, no death, no mortgage, no council tax, no income taxes, and certainly no rent. We will dwell in a mansion not made by human hands.

I just love talking about my Jesus, and you can't stop me from loving my God! I trust and depend on Him for protection throughout my Christian journey. What a friend! What a precious friend! He walks with me, talks with me, and tells me I am His own. Blessed assurance, Jesus is mine!

Some sweet day, I will be going home to be with my God and saviour. Jesus Christ. And what a meeting that will be: no more dying, no more crying. We will be free at last!

On the night when I gave my life to God, as I knelt at the altar, a voice said to me, *"Seek ye first the Kingdom of God and all his righteousness and all other things will be added"*.

In this life, it is a blessing to have good things added to you. If you have savings and do not earn interest, you will lose out on your capital, as what you could buy for a pound today will cost more by the time you withdraw your savings due to inflation.

What greater gift can you receive than having good things added to your life? Jesus Christ awaits your commitment to Him. Do not procrastinate, and do not let anyone – mother, father, husband, wife, or children – hinder you from giving your life to God.

Every person will have to account for their life on the day of judgment. What will your answer be?

Let it be now, and you will rejoice in giving your life to God. He is ever so faithful to all who are willing to surrender to Him. He loves us; it is our sins that He does not love. The whole duty of man is to serve God and keep His commandments.

To all who profess to be true Christians, let's pray for a worldwide revival. People need God in their lives. We might not be able to feed over five thousand on five loaves of bread and two fish, but I know a Man who can, and His name is Jesus Christ.

It is simply not right for some individuals to be unable to clothe and feed themselves while others have it all. What are you doing with millions in the bank while your fellow men and women are suffering severe hardships?

Remember, you cannot take your riches with you when you die. Do not wait until then to start dreaming of telling your family where you hid your wealth.

Make plans now; create a proper will and leave some to a good charity that seeks to help others. Do your best to be kind to others. When you help those in need, you are aiding God's children.

We are our brother's keeper. Give with love, and do not give sparingly. When you give in love, you will be rewarded by God. If you are running a business, it will grow by one hundred percent.

CHAPTER 10

POSTSCRIPT

My heart breaks to see what is going on around us today, and I sometimes wish I had the power to change things. And even though I am not a well-educated man, I have God with me.

As the father of six children, eight grandchildren, and three great-grandchildren, I realise that the world I will be leaving them is vastly different from the one into which I was born.

The records indicate that the 1930s were very depressing years. I remember the Second World War and the conditions of that time; yet even those days seem better than what we face today.

What can you and I do about it? Not much, but there is an answer to every situation in this life. We can all reach a place where we can call on God, and He will answer.

Over the years, through all the ups and downs, I can look back and say, "Thank you, God!" When I arrived in the United Kingdom, my first pay packet was £7.00 per week. At retirement, at the age of 70, my annual income was £21,000, and I was relieved to give up my job. Money cannot buy happiness.

God has been good to me, and I want to give Him praise for His goodness. I had a very loving mother who took great care of me from childhood. My father foolishly lost the opportunity to marry such a beautiful woman, yet I love him too. He recognised his mistakes and expressed his regrets in a letter he sent me years ago, lamenting that he had not helped me more.

He failed to provide child support, yet when I started working, I supported him until his passing. I even travelled to Jamaica to help respectfully bury him, and my final act was to return to Jamaica to install his headstone.

It does not matter what nationality you belong to; we are all God's handiwork.

I have shared incidents where women as young as 18 years old expressed a desire to have affairs with me, and I refused. A young woman once attempted to explain why women were so interested in me. According to her, it was akin to when Jesus was on earth; they wanted to be with Him because of the beauty within Him. But that was not by my own doing; it was the supernatural change that took place in me before I turned 18, when I committed my life to Jesus.

To all those who profess to be children of God: present your bodies as a living sacrifice, holy and acceptable to God! You cannot call yourself a born-again Christian and engage in affairs while you have a spouse.

My friend, it is wrong, and you must abandon this ungodly lifestyle; otherwise, you will face eternal damnation alongside the devil and his demons.

People often wonder why I speak differently from other men, and my answer is, "I am a child of God." I must walk right, act right, and speak right; my words must be my bond. I am a man, and there are times I feel weak, but keeping my eyes on Jesus enables me to say 'no' when tempted.

If Adam had been faithful, we would not find ourselves in this predicament. Had he refused to eat the fruit, the world would be much better off today. God would have dealt with Eve differently, and perhaps we would not have to die. Adam dared to tell God, "It is the woman You gave me who offered me the fruit to eat." The blame game is rampant today; we fail to take responsibility.

Today, many claim there is no God, but you are mistaken. The Holy Book states, "The fool says in his heart, 'There is no God.'" (Psalm 14:1). I once heard a preacher say, "There will be many educated fools in hell." Don't be one of them, my friend.

I know where I am going after my death; I am on my way to heaven, and I won't turn back. Throughout my time on this earth, I have met many wonderful people who have gone home to be with the Lord, and I long to meet them again!

I do not know when that time will come, but I am determined to make it. I simply do not want to go to hell when I die; I aspire to enter that mansion that our Lord has prepared.

A SPECIAL INVITATION

In 1951, just before my 18th birthday, I approached the church altar, knelt, and asked God to forgive me for all my sins. I made a promise to serve Him for the rest of my life. I invite you to join me and others who are on our way to a better life. Here is my heartfelt invitation to seek God and give Him your heart for the entirety of your life.

If possible, please kneel and pray as follows:

Lord Jesus, I know I have done wrong, and I have not shown the love that you have for me. I have sinned and become short of your glory and honour. The things I should have done, I failed to do so; the love I should have had for you, I have not had.

Please forgive me of all my sins. I now make a promise to serve you for the rest of my life, and at the end, be with you in the mansion you have promised when you were on earth.

O God, the Father of all mankind, please fill me with your Holy Spirit so I can overcome the plans of Satan. I know you love me, and that was why you sent your Son to die for my sins. I ask for your protection in the name of the Father, Son and Holy Ghost.

Now, if you have a Bible, please get it, or purchase one as soon as possible. Find these scriptures in the Holy Bible and read them repeatedly:

- 1 John 1
- Romans 12
- Ephesians 1
- Psalms 32

Hymns:

- Thank you, Lord, for loving me.
- I got Jesus right within my heart.
- I surrender all.
- At the cross where I first saw the light, the burden of my soul rolled away.
- I found the light.

- God will make a way.
- Nearer to the cross. You are my all in all.
- Lead me to the cross. You are my all. Lord, I have wandered far away; now I am coming home.
- Some glad morning when this life is over, I will fly away!
- Shine Jesus, shine.
- I promise to meet you by the river.

Can you make me a promise that you will meet me on the other side?

Thank you, and may the blessings of God be with you and comfort you in the name of Jesus Christ, His son.

God bless you, my friends.

BONUS SECTION

Interview with Mrs. Rita Hyatt

How are you doing, Ma'am?

I'm good forever. Thank God for that!

What was your first impression when you met Ronald Hyatt?

The first time I saw Ronald, well, my first impression was, he looked just like my dad! As a daughter, I love my dad so much, and he loves me so much, too. So, I felt I had found somebody who would suit me.

How did he come across to you as a person?

I must say he looked gentle and kind and caring, and when I spoke to him and listened to him talk, I knew we would get along together. Yeah, he was handsome, but that was not the most important thing because sometimes looks are deceiving, but when we sat down and talked, I got a better understanding of the person he was. I loved him for it.

How long have you been married?

We have been married for 65 years now. 65 years of marriage have taken a lot! Many do not even reach 5 years, but we have always been very committed to each other. We try to see eye-to-eye on issues and stand in the same space with each other. We pledged to live together as one until death. So, whatever comes, we just have to sort it out. We don't want our opinions to be one-sided, so we always try to listen to each other. We do sometimes have disagreements, but it's only God who does not make mistakes, so we find a way to rectify them without any brawl.

How did you cope, knowing that a lot of ladies were after him?

Yes, there were a lot of ladies after him everywhere he goes because he's a handsome chap! He always told me about them, but I was the one who was blessed to get him. He told me everything, and I have always trusted him.

You raised six children. How did you cope with parenting? Any tips for today's parents?

Well, you've got to know how to train them up the way they ought to go, and we were a close family. I was also brought up in a Christian home, so I was taught to be kind and sort things out. There were challenges at different times as they grew up, but we tried our best to sort them out.

What parenting advice would you give to parents today?

Oh, to be kind and gentle. Children will always be children, but as adults, we have to know which way to take them; otherwise, we will lose them. If that happens, we are the ones who will be losing, and the world will gain them. So, we must try our best and look to God to lead the way.

Is there any other thing you'd like to say about your husband?

He's loving and kind, and he loves the Lord. That's what I wanted in a man. And that's the reason we are still together after 65 years. God knows we had many ups and downs, but I know the love of God put into this man, and it has made him something.

What are some of your fondest memories in the last 65 years?

Oh, Memories! Going on holiday! He took me to many places that I wouldn't have gone. I miss them all now, but I can look back on many good days: going to church with the children, enjoying ourselves on those holidays. So many memories, and I still love it! But my memory is not so good now...

The last holiday we travelled, we went to Israel, to the spots where Jesus walked. It was wonderful, seeing where Jesus walked and did his works. That is one of the fondest memories I have.

How can believers today build lasting marriages and a home that glorifies God?

You've got to love each other and put God first. Whatever the problems you might have with your family. Your friends, neighbours and even your spouse, put it to the Lord and let him sort it out for you. Otherwise, you are in danger because you won't live a life to suits each other. God must be first in our lives. I learned that as a child growing up in Sunday school. I learned to love the Lord, and I have learned to love my husband, too.

Ronald's Footnote

Number one is issues of trust. Many years ago, we decided we were going to have a joint account. Both of us had what we called a post office account. When we decided to open a bank account, we went and put in about 200 pounds into the account. Back then, 200 pounds was a lot of money. Looking at the way we were going about it, the bank manager turned to us and asked, *"How do you want to set up this account: either or both?"* I asked him to explain what he meant, and he explained to me. I looked at her and told him, *"Yes, we will have a joint account such that even if I'm not at home, my wife will be free to go to the bank and withdraw some money".*

"You trust her?" and I replied, *"Yes, I do!"*

Those are the things that count. We are not going to say life is cool and smooth. There are ups and downs in life because we have an enemy who is a liar. Put your faith in God and let Him lead you.

That's what I would say to every young Christian. Let God lead you!

Printed in Dunstable, United Kingdom

68761900R00077